D1021978

Engel v. Vitale

Separation of Church and State

To Ken, Adam, and Jake

Engel v. Vitale

Separation of Church and State

Carol Haas

Landmark Supreme Court Cases

ENSLOW PUBLISHERS, INC.

44 Fadem Road	P.O. Box 38
Box 699	Aldershot
Springfield, N.J. 07081	Hants GU12 6BP
U.S.A.	U.K.

4014   57694   7-7-99
Library of Congress Cataloging-in-Publication Data

Haas, Carol.
    Engel v. Vitale: separation of church and state / Carol Haas.
       p. cm. — (Landmark Supreme Court Cases)
    Includes bibliographical references and index.
    ISBN 0-89490-461-2
    1. Engel, Stephen—Trials, litigation, etc.—Juvenile literature.
2. Vitale, William J.—Trials, litigation, etc.—Juvenile literature. 3. Prayer in the public
schools—Law and legislation—United States—Juvenile literature. 4. Religion in the
public schools—Law and legislation—United States—Juvenile literature. 5. Church and
state—United States—Juvenile literature. [1. Engel, Stephen—Trials, litigation, etc.
2. Vitale, William J.—Trials, litigation, etc. 3. Religion in the public schools.
4. Church and state.] I. Title. II. Title: Engel versus Vitale. III. Series.
    KF228.E54H33 1994
    344.73'0796—dc20   93-26381
    [347.304796]   CIP
                                                       AC

Printed in the United States of America

10 9 8 7 6 5

Photo Credits: A/P World Photos, p. 30; Collection of the Supreme Court of the
United States, pp. 72, 112; Carol Haas, pp. 8, 70; Library of Congress Collections,
pp. 55, 60; National Archives, pp. 14, 16, 18, 24, 40, 47, 79, 82, 93, 97, 103;
Supreme Court of the United States: Franz Jantzen, photographer, pp. 69, 114.

Cover Photos: Franz Jantzen, "Collection of the Supreme Court of the United
States" (background); Prints and Photographs Division, Library of Congress
(insert).

Contents

1

The Case That Shook a Nation

Imagine you are a student at a high school in New Hyde Park, New York, in the late 1950s. Each morning when the opening school bell rings and you scramble to your seat, you are greeted by an announcement over the public address system, asking you to rise, bow your head, and recite the twenty-two-word Regents' Prayer:

"Almighty God, we acknowledge our dependence upon Thee, and we beg Thy blessings upon us, our parents, our teachers, and our country." To most students, the prayer was just another part of opening exercises that followed the Pledge of Allegiance. And to the members of the Board of Regents who created the prayer, those twenty-two words that took eight seconds

Students in New Hyde Park bowed their heads every morning as part of their opening exercises. Despite the fact that this particular school district endorsed the prayer introduced by the Board of Regents, only a small percentage of school boards in New York State actually used the prayer.

to recite were simple and harmless, just a small part of a program introduced into the public schools to encourage stronger moral values in the classroom. No student was "required" to recite the prayer; students could stand in silence if they so chose. And local school boards had the option of adopting the prayer or not using it at all. To the members of the board, the prayer did not favor any one religious group and could not possibly offend anybody.

The Board of Regents could not have been more wrong. Five parents with a total of ten children in the New Hyde Park School District, near the New York City boundary, found the prayer so offensive that they filed a lawsuit against the local school board. The objecting parents had varied religious backgrounds. Two were Jewish; one was Unitarian, focusing on individual freedom of beliefs; another was a member of the Ethical Culture Society, which focuses on promoting social welfare through community efforts; and the fifth was an atheist or nonbeliever.

All of the parents argued that school prayer violated the First Amendment of the Constitution. This amendment prohibits the government from passing laws establishing a religion. And the prayer itself, they maintained, was contrary to their particular religious beliefs and practices.

9

One of the objecting parents was Stephen Engel. The chairman of the New Hyde Park School Board was William Vitale, Jr. The case came to be known as *Engel* v. *Vitale,* and some people referred to it as the "New York Regents' Prayer Case."

From the moment the five parents filed the lawsuit with the trial court in 1959, they and their children suffered the ordeal of hateful telephone calls, letters, and remarks in the classroom. School authorities were more than surprised when the Supreme Court of the United States agreed to hear this case. To the school district, the prayer was a small and insignificant issue.[1] After all, they reasoned, the prayer was voluntary. But the Court *did* agree to consider the case. Its final decision in the summer of 1962 sent shock waves across the country, setting off an explosion that would change the role of religion in the public schools for decades to come.

Little did these five parents know that their perseverance would set the stage for other court decisions relating to the separation of church and state in the next few years. Decisions that affected Bible-reading and recitation of the Lord's Prayer in public schools would also reach the United States Supreme Court.

The case of *Engel* v. *Vitale* challenged the public school system and the constitutionality of prayer. It also tested the strength and convictions of the parents and children who opposed the views of their friends and classmates and seven Supreme Court Justices. Who could have predicted that the ruling would become so unpopular with the general population and religious groups alike?

2

Separation of Church and State — History

The *Engel* v. *Vitale* case is based on the concept of separation of church and state, an idea embraced by Thomas Jefferson and James Madison. It is a belief that there should be a wall of separation between the government and each person's own private religious beliefs. The two should never overlap. The phrase "wall of separation" was first used by Thomas Jefferson. He used it to explain why he, as president, was prohibited by the First Amendment from declaring a national religious day of fasting. A religious ceremonial day approved by the federal government would cross over that wall of separation between church and state.

The lands that would become the United States were

Thomas Jefferson, the third president of the United States, introduced the phrase "wall of separation between church and state." The first phrase of the First Amendment includes that concept.

originally settled by colonists from England and Europe who were seeking religious freedom. This made separation of church and state an important part of the newly formed United States. The original Constitution, passed in 1788, mentioned religion only once—in Article VI. It stated that "no religious Test shall ever be required as a Qualification to any Office or Public Trust under the United States."

Many of the writers of our Constitution sensed that, as written, the Constitution would not provide full protection of many of the liberties they had fought so hard to achieve. So an agreement was made. The delegates would encourage passage of the Constitution, a Preamble, and seven articles, if amendments were added later specifically to protect personal freedoms.

The promises were kept and James Madison wrote twelve amendments, or additions, ten of which were passed in 1791. These became the "Bill of Rights."

Freedom of religion was the very first freedom provided in the First Amendment of the Bill of Rights. Other rights included in that amendment are freedom of speech, of the press, of assembly, and to petition the government. The other nine amendments in the Bill of Rights provide protections against unreasonable search and seizure, guarantees of a fair trial, protections for those charged with a crime, and the right to bear arms.

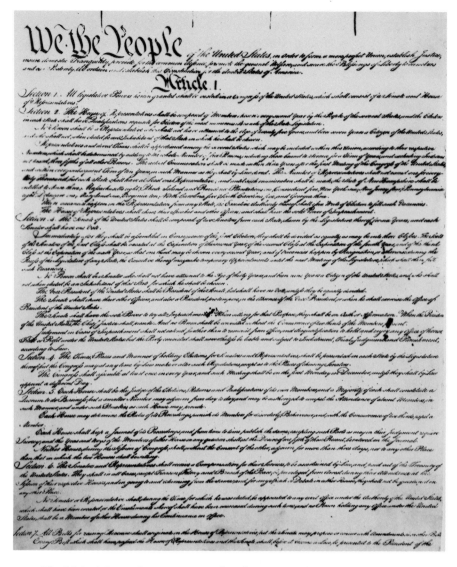

The United States Constitution made references to religion only once in its Preamble and seven articles. It was not until the First Amendment was passed in 1791 that the Founding Fathers talked about religious rights and freedoms.

The case of *Engel* v. *Vitale* revolved around the First Amendment guarantee of religious freedom. This amendment says, "Congress shall make no law respecting the establishment of religion, or prohibiting the free exercise thereof." Legal scholars have been confused by the meaning of those sixteen simple words for decades. Like the rest of the Bill of Rights, they are vague and can mean different things to different people.

For example, imagine that there is a speed limit law in your state that says: "No person shall drive a vehicle at a speed in excess of thirty miles per hour in any urban or residential area." That's very clear and leaves no room for a different interpretation. If you drive faster than thirty miles an hour in your neighborhood, you know you'll be breaking the law.

Compare this wording with the law that guarantees religious freedom in the First Amendment: "Congress shall make no law respecting the establishment of religion, or prohibiting the free exercise thereof." Or compare it with the words that provide freedom of speech: "Congress shall make no law . . . abridging the freedom of speech." These vague words leave us all, including United States Supreme Court Justices, with many questions. What constitutes the establishment of a religion? What is an abridgment of or decrease in our freedom of speech?

James Madison was one of the Founding Fathers who worked hard to provide Americans with freedom of religion and the other liberties included in the Bill of Rights.

The Bill of Rights is short and simple. It was intentionally designed to be flexible and open to interpretation. That means that the Founding Fathers did not want to predict what society would be like in decades, even centuries to come. By not making hard-and-fast rules, they allow each Justice to search his or her own conscience and determine what is best for the country and its people at that particular moment in time. Chief Justice Earl Warren once said that the Bill of Rights was intentionally written the way it was so that it "could function under constantly changing conditions—even those we have today and those we will have in generations to come."

The particular Justices sitting on the bench at any given time can determine how an amendment is viewed. If the *Engel* question was put to the Justices serving on the Supreme Court today instead of to the Justices on the "Warren Court" in 1962, they might rule differently.

How Does the First Amendment Guarantee Religious Freedom?

The guarantee of religious freedom in the First Amendment is made up of two parts:

The Establishment Clause prohibits the government from favoring one religion over another or from sponsoring a specific church or religion.

19

The Free-Exercise Clause prohibits the government from passing laws that place burdens on individuals because of their religious beliefs.

The two clauses are often in conflict. Together they state that no religion can be supported, but none can be inhibited or stifled either. It becomes the Court's job to balance the two clauses.

It was the Establishment Clause that created the concept of separation of church and state, and it was this clause that the Supreme Court examined in 1962 to determine the outcome of *Engel* v. *Vitale*. Judges, lawyers, and legal scholars have been trying to determine the meaning of the Establishment Clause since its beginnings, and there seem to be two different interpretations.

Some people believe that the clause only prohibits the government from using tax dollars to establish and support *one* official, national religion. If the Supreme Court had used this interpretation of the Establishment Clause, it would probably have allowed the Regents' Prayer, because this did not support or create one particular religion.

However, the second way of looking at the Establishment Clause is more restrictive. It says that this clause was intended to create an impenetrable wall separating church and state, with absolutely no government involvement in religion. It seems that the Supreme Court Justices in 1962 followed this interpretation.

The Justices had to look at two different things when they were trying to interpret the Constitution and *Engel* v. *Vitale.*

First, they had to determine what was the intention of the Founding Fathers of our country when they wrote the Constitution originally. That task was particularly difficult because public education did not exist at that time and there was no way to determine how the writers of the Constitution might have felt about school prayer. Second, the Justices had to consider whether the intent of the Founding Fathers would fit into today's society. Over a span of 200 years, the religious makeup of the country has changed. The number of different religions has increased and beliefs have become more varied. As Justice Brennan said in 1963, "practices which may have been objectionable to no one in the time of Jefferson and Madison may today be highly offensive to . . . the deeply devout and the non-believers alike."[1]

In reaching its decision in the *Engel* v. *Vitale* case, the Court did not only have to interpret the Constitution. It also had to look at the intent of those who created it and previous court decisions. These previous decisions are known as precedents. For these, the Justices didn't have to look back too far.

The debate over separation of church and state had really begun some fifteen years earlier. In 1947, a taxpayer named Everson in Ewing, New Jersey, sued the local government because it had allowed county money to be spent on school transportation. Parents had spent money on buses to transport their children to and from school, both public and religious schools, and the local government paid them back with money from taxes.

Mr. Everson felt that allowing tax money to be spent on busing children to private religious schools violated the Establishment Clause of the Constitution.[2] But the Court in Everson v. Ewing Board of Education decided in favor of the school system. It determined that providing transportation was a necessary service for the safety and well-being of the children; it did not benefit the religious schools themselves. This concept came to be known as the "child benefit theory." It was used in later cases by the Court to explain why it supported a religiously oriented activity.

The Justices who dissented, or disagreed with the majority opinion, said that providing the bus transportation violated the separation of church and state doctrine.

This was the first Supreme Court case that dealt with

the issue of separation of church and state. Even more importantly, the Court also declared for the first time that the states were required to provide the same guarantees of religious freedom as the federal government. (As originally passed in 1791, the Bill of Rights had placed restrictions only on the federal government. It was not until the Fourteenth Amendment went into effect in 1868 that the states were subject to the same restraints and obligations provided by the original ten amendments.) Justice Hugo L. Black wrote in the *Everson* majority opinion that the establishment of religion clause meant that neither the state nor the federal government could:

- Set up a church.

- Pass laws that aid one religion, all religions, or prefer one over another.

- Force a person to go or refrain from going to church or to profess a belief or disbelief in any religion.

- Punish an individual for his religious beliefs.

- Levy a tax to support any religious activity.

- Openly or secretly participate in the affairs of any religious organization or groups.

In his opinion, Justice Black stated that "the First Amendment has erected a wall between church and state.

Justice Hugo Black, on the bench of the United States Supreme Court from 1937 to 1971, was best known for his historic decisions and writings about freedom of religion in *Everson* v. *Ewing Board of Education* and later in *Engel* v. *Vitale.*

That wall must be kept high and impregnable. We could not approve the slightest breach."[3]

Should Religious Instruction Be Provided in Public Schools?

In 1948, Vashti McCollum of Champaign, Illinois, was unhappy because the public school that her son attended permitted children to receive religious instruction once a week. Clergy and religious instructors would come during usual school hours and provide instruction in school classrooms. Her son, one of those wishing to be excused from such instruction, was required to attend study halls elsewhere in the school while the religious classes were being held.

Mrs. McCollum sued the state of Illinois, arguing that tax money was being spent on these religious classes. After all, they were being held in public school buildings during regular school hours. The Supreme Court agreed, declaring the practice to be unconstitutional in the landmark case of *McCollum* v. *Board of Education*.

The case of *Zorach* v. *Clauson*, in 1952, dealt with a similar issue, but involved religious instruction that was being provided off school property. Those students who wanted religious instruction would be dismissed from class during regular school hours. Those students who preferred to remain at school would have a study period.

Those bringing the 1952 lawsuit argued that teachers "policed" the program and regular classroom work was stopped to release children for the religious instruction. This showed, they said, that the school was supporting the practice and placing influence on the children to participate in the program. The Court disagreed. It stated that school property was not being used, and that the children were not being forced to attend the religious instruction. Eliminating this "released-time" program would show hostility toward religion, said the Court.

These three cases, *Everson*, *McCollum*, and *Zorach*, paved the way for the Court's decision on school prayer in 1962. Although these decisions were important, it was the next one, *Engel* v. *Vitale*, that was to rewrite religious policy in the schools of the United States for decades to come.

3

Objections to the Prayer

Suppose your school day begins with a prayer led over the school intercom by the principal. Participation is not required, and you decide that prayer in school goes against the way you've been raised or what you believe—as the Engel children and the other families did. You have three choices:

- You can participate with the rest of the class and recite the prayer even though you don't agree with the meaning of the words.

- You can stand silently and not participate, without calling attention to yourself.

- You can excuse yourself from the classroom and stand in the hallway.

You may feel, as did some students in the *Engel* case,

that the first and second options are not really choices at all. They deny you your basic right to freedom of religion and they leave you without the right to make choices about the religious teachings you believe in. The parents in the *Engel* case believed that the third choice goes even further to violate your religious freedom. It calls attention to the fact that you worship differently from everyone else and that you don't follow the crowd. Worse yet, there's no guarantee that you won't have to hear the prayer since the intercom can be heard throughout the school. And if you were able to go to a location where the prayer was not heard, you might miss the school announcements.

These are the circumstances that prompted five parents of students in the New Hyde Park School District to file *Engel* v. *Vitale*. This lawsuit would eventually change the future, not only of prayer in the schools, but of Bible-reading and other religious exercises. The parents and students in the *Engel* case believed that an individual should not have to be faced with the alternatives of either tolerating a prayer that violated his or her religious beliefs or being singled out from the rest of the students.[1]

There were actually five parents who initiated the lawsuit: Lenore Lyons, Monroe Lerner, Stephen Engel, Daniel Lichtenstein, and Lawrence Roth. Engel's name was used first because when there is more than one person in a lawsuit, their names are listed alphabetically. The first name, in alphabetical order, becomes the representative for the case. The five parents had a total of ten children in the New Hyde Park Schools. They came from varied religious backgrounds—Jewish, Unitarian, the Ethical Culture Society, and atheist.

The atheist in the group of five parents, Lawrence Roth, ran an advertisement in the Nassau County newspapers, asking for other parents to come forward to join the crusade against school prayer. About fifty parents responded to his advertisement.

The families represented by Stephen Engel had the added support of several large and visible groups which later filed supportive written arguments called *amicus curiae* (which means "friend of the court" in Latin). These groups included the New York branch of the American Civil Liberties Union, the American Ethical Union, and the Synagogue Council, just to name a few. Another source of strong support came from nineteen Attorneys General, each state's highest lawyer, each of whom submitted a brief to the United States Supreme Court.

The initial lawsuit in 1959 was brought in New York State's major trial court, the New York Supreme Court. This case was tried in the state court system instead of the

These are members of the five families that sued the New Hyde Park School District in the case of *Engel* v. *Vitale*. They were subjected to ridicule, harassing phone calls, and hate mail because they took a stand against school prayer.

federal because it involved the question of whether a state law had violated the United States Constitution. Stephen Engel and the other four parents were the plaintiffs, or the ones with a complaint, in the case. The defendant was the New Hyde Park School Board that had introduced the prayer into the school. It was represented by the school board chairman, William Vitale, Jr. Using the name of a public official is often done when a governmental body is being sued. That individual is not held personally responsible, but is being sued as a representative of a given office, department, or agency.

The plaintiffs in the *Engel* case (parents and children) lost in the trial court, with the judges upholding the constitutionality of the state prayer. But they instructed the New York State Board of Education to make suitable arrangements for those students who preferred not to recite it.

Unwilling to accept the court's decision, Engel and the other parents took their case to a state appellate court. It, too, agreed with the trial court judges. Still not put off, Engel and the other parents went to New York's highest court, the Court of Appeals. Once again they were defeated. Its Chief Justice stated that the Court was going to uphold the prayer because "the belief and trust in a Creator has always been regarded as an integral and inseparable part of the fabric of our fundamental institutions." But the court did stress that students should not be forced to participate in the prayer if they or their parents objected to it.

The parents had taken their case as high as they could in the state court system. Their last resort was the highest court in the country, the United States Supreme Court.

The United States Supreme Court

The Justices of the United States Supreme Court decide among themselves which cases they are willing to hear. The number of cases they have to choose from is so overwhelming that they reject about 98 percent of those submitted to the Court for review every year.

The people submitting a case to the Supreme Court are no longer the plaintiffs or defendants. If you have lost in the lower court and are the party bringing the case, you are called the petitioner. So the parents became the petitioners and the school board became the respondents.

On December 4, 1961, the Justices of the United States Supreme Court agreed to hear the case of *Engel* v. *Vitale*. The lawyers from each side had about three months to write their arguments into a document called a brief. These would be filed with the Court. The Justices would then read these briefs and examine any other information available before oral arguments were presented in April of 1962.

Arguments Used by Engel and the Other Parents

Those fighting to have the Regents' Prayer banned had several reasons for their opposition:

1. Because saying the Regents' Prayer is a religious activity, it violates the doctrine of separation of church and state. The fact that the prayer was a religious activity was never disputed by any of the parties, not even the school board. Religious activities in the schools violate the First Amendment guarantee of religious freedom. They clearly involve government support and the advancement of an undisputable religious exercise.

2. The prayer was not voluntary. Students could choose to excuse themselves or merely not participate. But the peer pressure and expectations from the teachers made it almost impossible for a student to feel comfortable about refusing to join in the recitation.

3. A government that dictates the use of specific religious practices is committing the same abuses that European governments did in the 16th and 17th centuries.

To better understand the intent of those who wrote the Constitution and determine why the highest court in the land issued the bold decision it did, it is important to travel back in time to 1776. Actually, we could go back even further to 17th-century England where one church reigned supreme, the Church of England. The *Book of Common Prayer* set forth the only religious practices permitted in the country. Following any other beliefs was a criminal act. Minority religious groups, including the Puritans and Catholics, struggled for a voice in their country's religious life, but it was of no use. Feeling powerless, many looked across the ocean to the newly established colonies as homes where they would have the right to worship as they pleased.

Yet the lesson was lost on many of the colonists. When they arrived in their new homelands and found themselves in positions of power, they began establishing official religions in each of the colonies. For instance, in Maryland, Virginia, and North and South Carolina as well as Georgia the official church was the one the settlers had left behind, the Church of England. Pennsylvania became a haven for those seeking religious freedom.

But by the time the colonies won independence from Great Britain in the Revolutionary War, the quest for religious freedom was sparked once again. Minority religious groups, such as Quakers and Baptists, not only practiced their religions freely but were a dominant religious force in the new United States.

Thomas Jefferson and James Madison led the

campaign to prohibit the government from controlling religion. The concept of separation of church and state was born, which would be written into the First Amendment.

America came into being because colonists wanted religious freedom. Our Founding Fathers carefully wrote the Constitution to grant that freedom. It makes no difference whether religious beliefs are imposed at a national, state, or local school district level, the abuse is still the same. A prayer created and supported by a government violates the very essence of the spirit in which the United States was formed.

4. Teachers are public employees, paid by taxpayers. The prayer required less than thirty seconds of a teacher's time each day, but it was, nevertheless, an expenditure of tax dollars. This was a violation of the separation of church and state. An infringement of a constitutional right is an infringement regardless of the time it takes to carry it out. The teacher is an authority figure. By leading the prayer, she or he is implying approval and support of the prayer. Because the teacher is a government employee, support of the prayer is a violation of the First Amendment.

5. The prayer is clearly a Christian prayer, offensive to non-Christians and atheists. To those religions and sects that use different terminology and hold different beliefs,

the prayer can be very offensive. The words "Almighty God" are included in the prayer, professing a belief that atheists, agnostics, and other "nonbelievers" do not hold. To expect children to stand quietly while a prayer running contrary to their beliefs is recited violates their constitutional rights.

The frustration that began for Stephen Engel and the other parents and children in the late 1950s with the recitation of the Regents' Prayer ended in June of 1962. But there was a long battle before the case ever reached the nation's highest court. The members of the school board believed in the prayer—and the American public supported them.

4

Why the School Board Believed in the Prayer

In 1951, the New Hyde Park School Board directed the teachers in their school district to lead their students in the recitation of a twenty-two-word prayer. It was part of opening exercises along with the Pledge of Allegiance. The prayer had been created and approved by the New York State Board of Regents. The Board of Regents was (and is) a committee that was hand-selected by the state legislature. Its members served without pay and came from various religious, political, and economic backgrounds. They made the decisions that controlled education throughout the state of New York. They voted unanimously in favor of the twenty-two-word prayer in 1951.

Since the prayer was recommended by the Board of Regents and permitted by New York law, it came as quite a shock to William Vitale and the rest of the New Hyde Park School Board when their practice was questioned. They had strong legal arguments to support the continued use of the Regents' Prayer. After the lawsuit was filed, sixteen parents came forward to join the school board in support of the prayer. They provided their own legal counsel. And the Board of Regents contributed by filing an amicus curiae or "friend of the court" brief.

Defenses Used by the New Hyde Park School Board

1. The prayer was not religious instruction. All parties agreed that prayer is obviously religious in nature. This prayer, however, was not used for teaching or training in religious beliefs. It was merely a voluntary confession of faith, a right guaranteed by the First Amendment. The facts that the prayer is recited following the Pledge of Allegiance, it is repeated daily without any changes, and there is no commentary accompanying it, are evidence that the Regents' Prayer is not religious instruction.

2. Prayer is an important part of America's rich spiritual heritage. The Regents' Prayer merely acknowledges the existence of a God. References to "Almighty God," "Thy

Blessings," and "Our dependence upon Thee" occur in the most important documents of our country, including the Declaration of Independence, the Gettysburg Address, the national anthem, and the presidential oath of office. Coins are engraved with the words "In God We Trust." Each session of the United States Supreme Court and each house of Congress begins with a prayer. Prayer and religion are a part of the American tradition.

3. The prayer was not required. The prayer was meant to give those students who wanted to profess their faith the opportunity to do so, yet excuse those who did not. Every student had the right to refuse participation. Statistics showed that only 29 of the 4,500 students in the school district asked to be excused.

4. The prayer is short and trivial, not warranting the attention of the United States Supreme Court. The prayer is a harmless, unimportant part of opening exercises that should not warrant involvement by the highest court in the United States. It requires only thirty seconds to recite, hardly enough time to mean a great deal to anyone.

5. The prayer does not favor one religious denomination or sect. The phrases used in the short prayer are accepted

United States Representatives bow their heads to pray before the beginning of each session of Congress. This example was used as an argument by the New Hyde Park School Board in support of allowing prayer to begin each day in the public schools.

universally in most religions. No single religious faith is favored. Those finding that the prayer goes against their beliefs do not have to participate.

6. Juvenile delinquency is on the rise, and removing prayer from the schools worsens the problem. The prayer was instituted by the Board of Regents as part of a program to provide moral and spiritual training in the schools. Educators as well as parents were attempting to counteract the increase in juvenile delinquency. They believed that a school program that included a short prayer would help get children back on the right track.

Those on both sides of the issue believed they had valid arguments for and against banning the prayer in *Engel* v. *Vitale*. Now it was up to the United States Supreme Court.

5

The Decision

As the nine Supreme Court Justices filed into the courtroom on the morning of June 25, 1962, the tension in the air could be felt. One of the most historic religious decisions of the century was about to be announced. Anticipation grew as the minutes passed. It was the last day of the session before summer break, and the Justices still had not issued a ruling on the highly controversial school prayer case. The court had seventeen rulings to announce that day, and if *Engel* v. *Vitale* was not one of them, there would be a three-and-a-half month wait until it could be announced at the next session.

The announcement of the rulings was further delayed by a ceremony honoring Justice Hugo Black, who had served twenty-five terms on the United States Supreme

Court. Not only was Justice Black one of the most famous individuals ever to serve on the Court, but he was coincidentally the justice who would write the majority opinion in *Engel* v. *Vitale.*

Justice Hugo Black. Justice Black was named to the Supreme Court in 1937 by President Franklin D. Roosevelt. His Senate confirmation came quickly, five days later, with a vote of 63 to 16. But shortly thereafter, things took a turn for the worse in Justice Black's judicial career. Newspaper stories reported that at one time he had been a member of the Ku Klux Klan, a racist society. The accusation caused a public outcry and demands for his resignation.

Black made a public statement on the radio defending his honor and good name. He admitted that he had once been a member of the Klan, but that he joined only because he thought it would help his career as a Southern politician in the 1930s.[1] He said he harbored no prejudices, either racial or religious, and did not follow the bigoted teachings of the KKK. This was the one and only statement Black made about the accusations.

Shortly after that uproar, Black found himself the target of criticism that he was incompetent, lacking the intelligence to sit on the highest court in the country. But his years on the bench proved all his critics wrong. He displayed no prejudices and only the highest level of ability. He was a champion of First Amendment rights, often writing the majority opinion in religion cases, as he did in *Engel* v. *Vitale*.

The Vote. The actual voting on the Court's decision and writing of the opinions were completed weeks before the final announcement. The attorneys were required to submit their briefs, or written statements of the arguments used in their cases, about three weeks before oral arguments, the spoken presentations of their cases before the Justices. On April 3, 1962, attorneys for both sides of the case had presented the "oral arguments." Each attorney got only thirty minutes to speak.

The following week, the Justices met in the Court's conference room, in the strictest secrecy, to discuss the issues in the *Engel* case. They had to reach a majority decision on a case that would change the use of school prayer for decades to come.

Chief Justice Earl Warren presided over the Court in June 1962 when the historic decision came down. But he was not a stranger to controversy. His sixteen terms on the bench were filled with decisions that raised many eyebrows and shocked the legal community. As a champion of civil rights, Earl Warren showed concern for the poor, minorities, and those people charged with crimes. He was the one to write the majority opinion in

Brown v. *Board of Education,* the case that declared school segregation unconstitutional.

On June 25, 1962, the Justices announced that they had voted 6 to 1 in favor of banning the Regents' Prayer. Those voting the majority position against the prayer were Chief Justice Earl Warren, and Justices Hugo Black, William O. Douglas, Tom C. Clark, William J. Brennan, Jr., and John M. Harlan. Justice Potter Stewart was the only justice to disagree. Justice Byron R. White decided not to vote because he was a new appointee to the Court. And Justice Felix Frankfurter, who was about to retire because of illness, did not vote either.

Justice Black was assigned the task of writing the majority opinion, which explains why the case was decided in the way it was. Justice Douglas wrote a concurring opinion, a statement agreeing with that of the other Justices. Concurring opinions are written because a justice wants his or her views expressed individually or because of a desire to add specific reasons for voting the way he or she did. Justice Stewart wrote the dissenting opinion, which explained why he disagreed with the other Justices and why he felt that the prayer should be permitted.

The written opinions in a case such as this are of extreme importance. Justices will rely on the rulings and

These are the Justices who sat on the bench of the United States Supreme Court in 1962. First row, left to right: William O. Douglas, Hugo L. Black, Chief Justice Earl Warren, Felix Frankfurter, Tom C. Clark. Back row, left to right: Potter Stewart, John Marshall Harlan, William J. Brennan, Jr., Byron R. White.

language in these opinions in later years to justify decisions that they make in similar cases.

Justice Black Announces the Court's Decision

In their majority opinion, the Justices stated that the Regents' Prayer was unconstitutional because it involved the government's singling out a particular religious practice and "placing its official stamp of approval" on it. This was a direct contradiction to the Establishment Clause of the First Amendment which prohibits the government from sponsoring or favoring any religion. The government was never given the power to support any religious activity, said the Court. The mistreatment of citizens in sixteenth-century England in the name of religion was evidence of the conflict such support created. The Court said that prayer is a purely religious activity that should be left to the people, not the government.

The Court also dealt with the arguments made by those supporting the prayer. It admitted that when compared to the government's role in religion two hundred years ago in England, the prayer was insignificant. But, argued the Court, it was still a violation of a citizen's rights, regardless of the prayer's length or importance. And although it took only thirty seconds of a teacher's time to lead the prayer, it was still public monies that paid his or her salary, and thus constituted financial governmental support of a religious activity.

Prayer supporters had argued that students were not forced to recite the prayer, and that it was strictly voluntary. Justice Black responded by saying that any time government places its power, prestige, and financial support behind a particular religious belief, the belief is no longer voluntary.[2]

Justice William O. Douglas wrote a concurring opinion, one that agreed with Justice Black's, but went surprisingly further. He stated that the prayer amounted to the government's financing a religious activity because repeating the prayer required time from the teachers whose salaries came from tax money. He concluded that this was unconstitutional. He caught the nation off guard when he listed other common practices that he thought were also unconstitutional, including:

- Holding religious services at federal hospitals and prisons.
- Engraving the slogan "In God We Trust" on coins.
- Using the Bible for the administration of oaths.
- Providing exemptions from income taxes for churches.

Concerned that the public might misread Justice

Douglas's concurring opinion as the majority decision, Justice Black made it very clear that the Court was not declaring these activities to be unconstitutional.

Justice Stewart, the only justice voting to uphold the prayer, wrote in his dissenting or disagreeing opinion that the Regents' Prayer did not constitute the establishment of an "official religion." And, he added, instead of looking at the mistreatment of people in 16th-century England because of religion, we should be looking at the American tradition reflected in practices that occur today. These include offering prayers before each session of the Supreme Court and Congress, as well as singing the national anthem, reciting the Pledge of Allegiance, and the president's proclamation of a National Day of Prayer, all of which concern some form of religious practice.

Justice Stewart quoted a Supreme Court decision from 1952: "We are a religious people whose institutions presuppose a Supreme Being."[3] He meant that religion is at the core of America, and that government was built on the belief that there is a higher power than mankind. To deny schoolchildren the chance to recite the prayer, he wrote, is denying them the opportunity of "sharing in the spiritual heritage of our Nation."

The religious backgrounds of the seven Justices had little or no apparent effect on their decision. Chief Justice Warren and Justice Black were Baptists; Justices Clark,

Harlan, and Douglas were Presbyterians; and Justice Brennan was a Roman Catholic. The only justice voting in favor of the prayer, Justice Stewart, was an Episcopalian.

None of the Justices could have dreamed of the impact their decision would have on the country, but they were about to find out.

6

Unexpected Reaction

The Court's decision regarding school prayer in 1962 took Americans by surprise. Newspapers were flooded with angry letters from readers. Politicians and religious leaders alike called the decision "shocking" and "tragic." And, whether they were Democrat or Republican, most members of Congress didn't like it.[1] North Carolina Representative Roy A. Taylor wasted no time in suggesting a constitutional amendment. He supported a change to the existing Constitution, stating that prayers could be recited and the Bible read in the public schools. In addition, Representative L. Mendel Rivers of South Carolina angrily accused the Court of "officially stating its disbelief in God Almighty" by its decision.[2]

Former politicians also reacted strongly. Former

President Herbert Hoover, who served from 1929 to 1933, called the Court's decision a "disintegration of a sacred American heritage." He demanded that Congress submit a constitutional amendment establishing the right to prayer.[3] Former President Dwight Eisenhower, who served from 1953 to 1961, said that he believed the United States has essentially always been a religious nation, and that even the Declaration of Independence deals with religious ideas by stating that it is "our common creator" that has given us certain individual rights and liberties.[4]

Then-President John F. Kennedy, was a bit more diplomatic and less critical. He merely stated that the Court was within its rights to decide as it did. He suggested, however, that the solution for those who oppose the decision would be to "pray ourselves, and I would think it would be a welcome reminder to every American family that we can pray a good deal more at home and attend our churches with a good deal more fidelity."[5]

Needless to say, the religious community was in an uproar. Protestants were split, some strongly supporting the ban, others seeing it as a threat to democracy.[6] Evangelist Billy Graham said that he was shocked and disappointed by the decision, calling it "a most dangerous trend."[7] He added that if it were "followed to its logical

John F. Kennedy was president when the *Engel* v. *Vitale* decision was announced. He attempted to calm the country by suggesting that the banning of school prayer could be counteracted with more prayer at home and more frequent attendance at church.

conclusion, prayers cannot be said in Congress, chaplains will be taken from the armed forces, and the president will not place his hand on the Bible when he takes the oath of office." Obviously, these predictions have not come true, but the decision did cause concern about the future of "godliness" in government.

Dean Kelley, a director of the National Council of Churches, saw merit in the Court's ruling, saying that many Christians would welcome it. "It protects the religious rights of minorities and guards against the development of 'public school religion' which is neither Christianity or Judaism but something less than either."[8]

The Catholic Church, however, saw nothing positive about the ruling. New York's Cardinal Spellman said that it "strikes at the very heart of the godly tradition in which America's children have for so long been raised."[9] Other cardinals saw it as communism sneaking into American culture. Boston's Cardinal Cushing asked his congregations to imagine to what extent the Communists would use that decision as a method of propaganda. Los Angeles's Cardinal McIntyre described the decision as "scandalizing" and "placing shame on our faces as we are forced to emulate Mr. Khrushchev."[10]

But just as strongly as the Catholic Church opposed the decision, Jewish leaders applauded it. A. M. Sonnabend, president of the American Jewish Committee, remarked that it "affirmed that prayer in our democratic society is a matter for the home, synagogue, and church, and not for state institutions."[11] And then there was the reaction from those directly involved in the lawsuit. The Board of Regents of the State of New York announced that schools throughout the state would honor the Court's new position on school prayer. William Vitale, Jr., the president of the New Hyde Park School Board when the lawsuit was filed, felt sure that those in charge would go along with the decision, but defended the use of the prayer. He stated that "at no time did we ever insist that a child should say it. We set up mechanics so no one would be compelled to say it and we felt sincerely we were not infringing on anyone's constitutional rights."[12]

Did the Schools Obey?

Although many teachers and administrators said they would comply with the United States Supreme Court decision regarding the Regents' Prayer, some decided to develop their own prayer and disregard the high court's ruling. Some schools attempted to get around the banning of prayer by creating verses that left out the words "God" or "Jesus Christ." In 1965, some Illinois schools allowed their kindergarten schools to recite a popular prayer with the word "God" removed from the last line:

> We thank you for the flowers so sweet;
> We thank you for the food we eat;
> We thank you for the birds that sing;
> We thank you for everything.

A group of parents sued the school district, and a federal district court ruled that the verse was not religious and did not violate the First Amendment. Still not content, the parents appealed the case to the Circuit Court of Appeals, where the judges reversed the federal court decision. With or without the word "God," the verse was still a prayer and still unconstitutional.

But what about silent prayer or a moment of silence? Some teachers, administrators, and parents were unsure whether these were permissible. Generally speaking, courts have permitted schools to provide a moment of meditation at the beginning or end of a school day. But students cannot be told to recite a "prayer." A 1976 Massachusetts ruling made it clear that state laws cannot provide children with the choice of either silent meditation *or prayer.*

But what if a group of students decide among themselves to hold a prayer session? The Supreme Court has never issued a ruling on that specific point. But it indicated its dislike for that, too, when it chose not to take an appeal from a lower court. The appeal dealt with a decision that declared student-initiated prayers to be just as unconstitutional as those endorsed by teachers or a school.

Congressional Reaction: The Becker Amendment

Congressional reaction to the school prayer decision was strong and swift. New York Republican Congressman Frank J. Becker called it the most tragic decision in the history of the United States.[13] He immediately introduced a constitutional amendment that would permit voluntary prayer in government or public schools. He introduced another amendment a year later after the Court issued a ruling stating that Bible-reading was not permitted in the schools.

Unfortunately for Becker, his amendment, promoting both prayer and Bible-reading in the schools, had an uphill battle for passage. The House Judiciary Committee was chaired by Emanuel Celler from Brooklyn, New York. He was opposed to religion in the schools. In fact, upon learning of the decision in the *Engel* case, Congressman Celler said he thought the Court had no other choice than to ban the prayer because it violated the First Amendment.

The House Judiciary Committee is one of the most

New York Republican Congressman Frank J. Becker dedicated years of congressional service to passing a constitutional amendment that would allow school prayer. Despite a great deal of support, his efforts were unsuccessful.

powerful standing, or permanent, committees in the House of Representatives. Its members have the power to "table" a law. This, in effect, kills or delays it. Committee members can also set the process in motion for the law to go to the full House for a vote.

Through the persistence of Congressman Becker, hearings were held before the House Judiciary Committee for eighteen days. The committee heard testimony from religious leaders, politicians, and lawyers. The response from the public was overwhelming. The committee and Chairman Celler received about 13,000 pieces of mail regarding a school prayer amendment. About 8,000 favored it and 5,000 opposed it.[14]

It is believed that the primary cause of defeat for Becker's amendment was the testimony of more than 220 constitutional law professors who argued that amending the Bill of Rights was unconstitutional. They maintained that the purpose of the Bill of Rights was to provide basic fundamental rights without interference from elections and majority votes. An authority on the First Amendment and the attorney for the Synagogue Council, Leo Pfeffer, commented that "if you open the door for constitutional amendments because a particular decision at a particular time is unpopular, the entire purpose of the Bill of Rights to ride out periods of passion will have been destroyed."[15]

But not everyone agreed with the feeling that the Bill of Rights could not be amended. The highest-ranking Republican member of the Judiciary Committee, Congressman William McCullough, believed that if the "patriotic, intelligent, and far-seeing forefathers" who wrote the Bill of Rights thought it was "sacred or untouchable," they would have specifically included that in the document.[16]

Becker was not the only member of Congress to take action against the *Engel* decision. By the end of the congressional session in 1964, one hundred fifty-one resolutions supporting prayers had been introduced by one hundred fifteen legislators from the House of Representatives. The Senate introduced eleven of their own.[17]

There were two other major efforts to pass prayer amendments during the next decade. After Congressman Becker's attempts in 1962 and 1963, followed by the hearings in 1964, nothing happened again in Congress until 1966. Senate Majority Leader Everett L. Dirksen, a Republican from Illinois, introduced a voluntary prayer amendment. His version specifically prohibited a government officer from dictating what was to be included in the prayer. A two-thirds vote of the Senate was necessary for the amendment to pass that house. It fell nine votes short.

Over the next five years, the prayer issue became less important as other issues took priority. But it was not forgotten. Two weeks after his historic Apollo orbit around the moon with fellow astronauts William Anders and James Lovell, Jr., Frank Borman addressed a special session of Congress. It included members of the United States Supreme Court. Borman joked about the fact that his fellow astronaut William Anders, a Roman Catholic, read from a Protestant version of the Bible as they orbited the moon on Christmas Eve, 1968. "One of the things that was truly historic was that we got that good Roman Catholic Bill Anders to read from the King James Version," said Borman. "But now that I see the gentlemen here in the front row," he said, referring to the Justices, "I am not sure that we should have read the Bible at all."[18]

A powerful petition drive in 1971 rekindled congressional interest in the prayer issue. Ohio Congressman Chalmers Wylie introduced an amendment, but it failed two-thirds passage by twenty-eight votes.

7

Bible-Reading and Saluting the Flag

Should Bible-Reading Be Permitted in the Schools?

Those passionately opposed to the *Engel* decision couldn't help but ask, "If school prayer is banned, can Bible-reading and the saluting of the flag be far behind?" And their question was answered.

At the time of the *Engel* v. *Vitale* decision, the reading of the Holy Bible in public schools was a common practice, even more so, in fact, than the recitation of a prayer. At least 40 percent of all schoolchildren listened to a daily reading from the Bible. Bible-reading was required in Alabama, Arkansas, Delaware, Florida,

Georgia, Idaho, Kentucky, Maine, Massachusetts, Mississippi, New Jersey, Pennsylvania, and Tennessee. In Colorado, Indiana, Iowa, Kansas, Maryland, Michigan, Minnesota, New York, North Dakota, Ohio, Oklahoma, and Tennessee it was permitted but not required.

But that's not to say the practice was unquestioned. Six states had already determined that it was unconstitutional to read the Bible in public schools—Illinois, Louisiana, Nebraska, South Dakota, Washington, and Wisconsin. And six other states were in the process of testing it in their courts.

And it was the Protestant Bible that was usually used in the schools—the King James Version. Objections came from Catholics (who used the Douay Version) and Jews (who followed the Old Testament, not the New Testament).

The Schempp Family. In the early 1960s, a Pennsylvania law required the public school day to begin with the reading of at least ten verses from the Bible. If parents didn't want their child to participate, they could be excused from the ten- or fifteen-minute exercise. Edward Schempp, a Pennsylvania electrical engineer, and his wife Sidney, as well as their children, Roger, Donna, and Ellory, felt that the reading of the Bible in public schools violated their Unitarian Church beliefs. The family belonged to the Unitarian Church in

Germantown, near Philadelphia, and the children were students at Abington Senior High School.

Each morning between 8:15 and 8:30 A.M., opening exercises were conducted and broadcast over the intercom system. These opening exercises included a reading from the King James Version of the Bible, recitation of the Lord's Prayer, the Pledge of Allegiance, and the daily school announcements. Ellory, the oldest Schempp child, protested by refusing to stand up during recitation of the Lord's Prayer. He also read a copy of the Islamic sacred book, the Koran, during the reading from the Bible. By the time the case made it to the Supreme Court, Ellory had graduated from high school and was no longer involved in the lawsuit.

His parents sued the Abington School District in federal district court. While testifying at their first trial, the Schemmps stated that Bible-reading and saying the Lord's Prayer violated their religious beliefs. This was unconstitutional. They maintained that their children would be embarrassed and treated differently if they asked to be excused from the classroom during opening exercises. They would also miss out on hearing the important school announcements that followed the exercises. The Schempps were successful in the trial court. But the school district appealed to the United States Supreme Court.

The Murray Family. While the Schempps were fighting Bible-reading in Pennsylvania, Mrs. Madeline Murray and her son, Bill, both atheists, had the same battle going on in Maryland. Bill was a student at Woodbourne Junior High School in Baltimore where prayer was required. No one could be excused from class. The Murrays gained national attention when Bill protested by "skipping" school for eighteen straight days. The Murrays managed to have the rule changed to allow students to be excused, but their fight was far from over. They refused to stop until the prayer and Bible-reading were banned completely.

The Murrays argued that showing children that moral values are directly related to religious beliefs makes the values of atheists appear to be immoral or of a lesser standard. The Murrays challenged a school board law in the state trial court and in the state court of appeals. Both courts ruled that the law was constitutional. So the Murrays took it to the United States Supreme Court. It arrived there at just about the same time as the Schempps' appeal, so the Court decided to combine both cases and issue one ruling.

In that ruling, the Supreme Court Justices voted 8 to 1 in favor of outlawing Bible-reading and saying the Lord's Prayer in public schools. Just one year before, the Court had declared the twenty-two-word New York

Regents' Prayer to be a violation of the Establishment Clause, so it was no great surprise when Justice Tom C. Clark announced the majority decision on June 17, 1963. Justices Douglas, Arthur Goldberg, Harlan, and Brennan all wrote concurring opinions. The Justices relied on the reasoning in previous decisions, particularly in *Engel.* Conducting a religious exercise in the schools cannot be done without violating the neutrality of government. The Court stated that there are times when the study of the Bible or of religion is acceptable. But the practice of reading the Bible in this case was a religious exercise and violated the First Amendment.[1]

Is Saluting The Flag Permissible in Schools?

Although saluting the American flag in school wouldn't seem to be a religious issue, it became one. In Pennsylvania during the 1930s and 1940s, a law required students to salute the flag and recite the Pledge of Allegiance. Two children, twelve-year-old Lilian Gobitis and her ten-year-old brother William, refused to participate in the flag ceremony. They argued that it violated their religious beliefs. They were Jehovah's Witnesses, and the salute and recitation of the pledge violated one of the basic principles of their Ten Commandments: "Thou shalt have no other Gods before me."

The school prayer decision in *Engel* v. *Vitale* paved the way for cases challenging the salute of the flag at school.

Jehovah's Witnesses are a Christian sect, founded in 1872 in Pittsburgh, Pennsylvania. The sect stresses the importance of the Bible and strictly follows its teachings. Their members, each of whom is considered a minister, go from door to door, handing out pamphlets to educate others about their religion. Jehovah's Witnesses believe that Jesus became king of all mankind in 1914 and will ultimately lead the forces of God to defeat Satan. They believe that this victory at the Battle of Armageddon will begin the one-thousand-year reign of Jesus, during which the dead will rise and be given a chance to embrace Christ. Satan will return at the end of Jesus Christ's reign, only to be destroyed along with his supporters.[2]

Witnesses hold fast to the principles laid down in the Ten Commandments, particularly to the belief that Jesus Christ is the Lord, and that no other gods should be placed before him. Showing allegiance to the United States, by saluting the flag, serving in the armed forces, or even voting, violates their religious beliefs.

When the Gobitis children were expelled for refusing to salute the flag, they were forced to attend a private school. Their parents sued the state of Pennsylvania. They not only asked the Court to declare the mandatory flag salute as unconstitutional but also asked to be compensated for the tuition that they were forced to pay

This is the courtroom of the United States Supreme Court. The nine Justices sit at the bench and the attorneys stand before them when it is their turn to present their oral arguments. This picture shows an empty courtroom because Court rules prohibit the taking of any photographs when the Justices are seated or when the Court is in session.

at the private school when their children were expelled from their public school.

In 1940, the Supreme Court in *Minersville School District* v. *Gobitis* decided in favor of the school. It stated that the act of pledging allegiance had neither directly promoted nor restricted religious activities.

Three years later, the Supreme Court changed its mind, in *West Virginia State Board of Education* v. *Barnette*, another flag salute case. In West Virginia during the 1940s, all students were required to salute the flag and recite the Pledge of Allegiance. Refusing to do so resulted not only in expulsion, but also in possible imprisonment and a fine for the parents. Some Jehovah's Witnesses families managed to get a court to issue an injunction. This would stop the school board from enforcing the law. An injunction is a formal command from the court ordering an individual or, in this case, a school board, to stop doing something which is causing damage.

The state of West Virginia appealed the decision to the United States Supreme Court. Ironically, on Flag Day of 1943, the Court declared that it was reversing the decision made in the *Gobitis* case. It declared mandatory flag saluting not only to be an infringement of religious rights but of personal rights as well. The Court ruled that to believe that patriotism will not grow and prosper if patriotic ceremonies are only voluntary instead of something that is required is to underestimate the minds of Americans.[3]

The Court concluded with the thought that if there is any "fixed star in our constitutional constellation," it is that no government can tell us what is proper in politics or religion.

8

Religious Issues in School

Prayers and Bible-reading are the most obvious religious influences in the schools. Yet there are many other spiritually oriented activities that courts have been called upon to either ban or declare permissible. One element of religion that can't be ignored is that some sects have particular practices or restrictions that conflict with those of the rest of society. It sometimes becomes a balancing act to protect the individual's First Amendment rights and the compelling interests of the state.

Do Students Have the Right to Attend a Private or Church-Related School?

A student's right to attend a private or church-related

school wasn't established until 1925. An Oregon law, passed in 1922, required students to attend public schools through the twelfth grade. A private Catholic school, the Society of Sisters, sued the state for interfering with its right to provide a private education. The school argued that parents had the right to select schools that would provide religious training in addition to the usual courses.

The church school argued that its right to conduct a business and own property was being violated by the state law requiring attendance at a public school, which was "arbitrary, unreasonable, and unlawful interference."[1] And, the church argued, not only would its particular school be destroyed, but so would all private elementary schools in Oregon.

The Supreme Court agreed with the school. It stated in its decision that the Oregon law was interfering with the rights of the school to run a business, as well as with the parents' rights to raise their own children. "The child is not the mere creature of the state; those who nurture him and direct his destiny have the right, coupled with the high duty to recognize and prepare him for additional obligations."[2]

Can Students Be Educated at Home Instead of in Schools?

Throughout the twentieth century there have been cases

in which parents have challenged school attendance laws. They believed that the free-exercise rights of the children were being violated by requiring attendance in a formal school setting. The courts have disagreed, arguing that the state itself must sometimes act as a child's parent or guardian if his or her well-being is jeopardized.

Such a case made it to a Virginia court in 1948, when the Rice family fought for the right to teach their children in their own home instead of sending them to school. Neither parent was a certified teacher, but they argued that the Bible supported education in the home. The Virginia Supreme Court ruled against the parents. It stated that children should not have to suffer by inferior education over a lifetime just because of the parents' dedication to religion.[3]

The only instance in which the United States Supreme Court made an exception to mandatory school attendance was in 1972 in the *Wisconsin* v. *Yoder* case of an Amish family. The Yoders were Old Order Amish, the most conservative group within the religious sect. Old order Amish people dress entirely in black, using hooks and eyes to fasten their clothing because buttons would be too ornamental. Amish men have beards and refuse to drive cars, relying on horse-drawn carriages for transportation. The Amish live by farming. They believe that all education after the eighth grade should be conducted in the home rather than in formal school systems.[4] The Yoders argued that mandatory school attendance interfered with their legitimate religious beliefs. The Court determined that in order for the state to force public education on the Yoder family and other Amish, it would have to show that the Yoders' free-exercise rights were not being violated or that the state interest was greater than their individual rights.

The Court ultimately ruled in favor of the Yoders and other Amish families. It stated that these children want to be prepared for a farm life that is separated from modern society. Since education in their own community would best provide this, the Court allowed this exception to mandatory attendance.

Can the State Require Students to be Vaccinated?

Vaccinations against childhood illnesses such as diphtheria and whooping cough are required by every state before a child can enter kindergarten. But some religions are morally opposed to vaccinations or medical treatment of any kind.

In New Hampshire during the 1930s, one parent refused to allow his child to be vaccinated. He gave religious reasons and said he didn't want "poison" injected into his child. The appellate court declared that

The Amish, who lead a very strict and simple farming existence, went to the Court to prove that they had the constitutional right to educate their children at home.

despite the parent's religious objections to the vaccination, his child's lack of immunization could endanger all the other schoolchildren. Over the years some states have permitted exemptions for those with religious objections. But many state Supreme Courts have determined that these exemptions are unconstitutional.

The Supreme Court of Mississippi did so in 1979. It declared that since immunizations were designed to equally protect the welfare of all children, religious exemptions violate this constitutional guarantee. The parents looked to the United States Supreme Court to change the lower court's ruling, but the high court refused to hear the case.

Can Schools Require Students to Take Courses That Violate Their Religious Beliefs?

Sometimes courses required by public schools can offend the religious beliefs of students and their families. In 1921, one family objected to their daughter's participation in a folk-dancing class in a California school. They argued that dancing violated their children's religious beliefs. The state appeals court ruled that the children should be permitted to excuse themselves from the dancing class.

In 1962, a female high school student in Alabama refused to participate in physical education class because she felt that both the exercises and the gym clothing she was required to wear were "immoral." When she was suspended from school, her parents filed a lawsuit in an Alabama trial court. The court declared that the girl should not be required to wear the clothing or participate in those activities that went against her religious beliefs.

But her parents were still unhappy. They said she would be like a "speckled bird," looking different from everyone else by wearing different gym clothing and not participating in certain activities.[5] They also argued that she was still subjected to looking at other girls in her class dressed in "immoral" outfits. They took their case to the Alabama Supreme Court, demanding that special physical education classes be provided to their daughter and others with similar beliefs. Once again they lost. The court stated that embarrassment must be accepted when one chooses a set of beliefs different from the majority.

In 1978, students who were of the Pentecostal faith refused to participate in coeducational physical education classes (boys and girls mixed) because the gym clothing was "immodest." Pentecostal churches teach that every Christian child should seek to be filled with the Holy Spirit. The students, who were short of enough credits to graduate because of physical education classes they

A girl in Alabama sued the state for requiring female high school students to wear clothing that she and her parents considered to be immoral.

missed, sued the state of Illinois in federal district court. This court issued a ruling different from the "speckled bird" case sixteen years earlier in Alabama. It stated that the physical education class *did* violate their free-exercise rights and that other accommodations could have been made. Other arrangements could include a separate gym class for the Pentecostal students or no gym class requirement at all.

In the early 1970s during the Vietnam War era, many schools required male high school students to take military training. In the Memphis, Tennessee schools, all male students were required to participate in either physical education or military training for one year. At one Memphis school physical education was not available, so male students had no choice but to sign up for military training. One student sued the school board, arguing that his religious beliefs were violated by training for the military. The Sixth Circuit Court of Appeals ruled that the state had no compelling reason to train students whose religious beliefs were in disagreement with those of the military.

A case two years later in Georgia ended differently. A student objected to participating in military training on the grounds that his right to freely exercise his beliefs—not necessarily his religious beliefs—had been violated. Since his objections had nothing to do with religion, said the Court, his First Amendment rights were not violated and he had no valid reason for avoiding military involvement.

Can Schools Be Required to Teach Creationism Instead of Evolution?

An even more explosive and well publicized issue than dancing and military training was the debate over whether the theory of evolution or creationism should be taught in the schools. Creationism is a theory that the universe was created by God exactly as set out in Genesis, the first book of the Bible. The theory of evolution is a scientific theory stating that all living things have gradually developed from more primitive life forms over millions of years.

In 1925, a Tennessee law required teachers to teach the theory of creationism. One teacher, whose name was John Scopes, taught the theory of evolution instead. After one of the most famous trials of this century, John Scopes was convicted and fined $100. But he appealed his case to the state supreme court, where it was reversed. The case never went to the United States Supreme Court and the state law was not taken off the books.

Forty-three years later, the Supreme Court finally had an opportunity to rule on the issue in *Epperson* v. *Arkansas*. A biology teacher tested the constitutionality of an Arkansas state law prohibiting state-funded schools from teaching the evolution theory. In 1968, the Court ruled that this law, which in effect required schools to teach the lessons of the Book of Genesis, violated the Constitution.

Nearly two decades later, the high court struck down a Louisiana law that required public school teachers to give the same amount of time and emphasis to the theory of creationism as to evolution. The Court found that the law was advancing "the religious viewpoint that a supernatural being created humankind."[6]

Can the State Provide Textbooks, Teacher Salaries, and Other Financial Aid to Religious Schools?

The question of whether state tax money could be used to provide schoolbooks and other financial help to private and religious schools was an issue as early as 1930. Taxpayers in Louisiana said that the use of public monies for this purpose amounted to the taking of private property (money from taxpayers) for a private purpose (religious-school students). The state supreme court disagreed in *Cochran* v. *Board of Education*. It stated that it was not the schools that benefited from the textbooks—only the children and the state. The United States Supreme Court agreed.

The issue arose again in 1968 in New York. Taxpayers challenged a similar law that provided textbooks to public and private school students alike. Once again the courts sided with the state. They reasoned that the law provided a program where the state continued to own the books. They were merely loaned to the students. "Thus no funds or books are furnished to parochial schools, and the financial benefit is to parents and children, not to schools."[7]

Another textbook case, in 1971, provided more guidelines for the states. A Pennsylvania taxpayer named Alton Lemon brought a lawsuit to prevent the state from paying private schools for textbooks and teachers' salaries. In its ruling, the United States Supreme Court stated that total separation between church and state was impossible. The Justices pointed out that fire inspections, building and zoning regulations, and school attendance laws were just a few examples of how the state must become involved in church-related activities. The line can easily become blurred between church and state.

The Court in *Lemon* then stated that an activity must meet three criteria to be sure the Establishment Clause is not violated. The government action must:

1. Not have a religious governmental function.
2. Neither advance nor inhibit religion.
3. Not support the government becoming excessively entangled with religion.

These three elements, which came to be known as the "Lemon test," were used by the Supreme Court for the next several decades to determine whether a law violated the Establishment Clause. The Court started looking to other criteria only in the mid-1980s.

The question of whether a state could constitutionally provide counseling and testing to religious schools became an issue in the 1977 Supreme Court case of *Wolman* v. *Walter.* The high court ruled that if a state provided standardized testing and grading to the public schools, it had to provide the same to the parochial schools. The Court also ruled that the state could give counseling to parochial school students, but that it had to be provided off the school property. On school grounds, the state was permitted to perform speech, hearing, and other kinds of diagnostic testing. But any money flowing to parochial schools from the state to pay for field trips had to stop; according to the Supreme Court this was unconstitutional.

Can Parents Receive Tax Credits for Their Children's Attendance at a Private School?

In 1983, a Minnesota law allowed parents to take a state income tax deduction for the expenses they incurred for school tuition, books, and transportation to school. The Supreme Court in *Mueller* v. *Allen* determined that since all parents, whether their children attended public or private schools, had the same opportunity to take the deduction, it did not violate the Constitution.

Can Religious Symbols Be Banned From Schools?

Plaques listing the Ten Commandments were often found in public schools. Parents in several states filed lawsuits attempting to have them removed because of their religious nature.

In 1978, the state of Kentucky passed an interesting law. It required that each school have a copy of the Ten Commandments posted in all classrooms. They were to be financed by private contributions to the state. Each wall display of the Ten Commandments had to be a specific size and had to have specific language at the bottom: "The secular application of the Ten Commandments is clearly seen in its adoption as the fundamental legal code of Western Civilization and the

Common Law of the United States."[8] This sentence was meant to imply that the Commandments were more of a universal law rather than religious teachings.

In response to a parent's lawsuit, the trial court concluded that the law requiring the posting of the Commandments was constitutional. Its teachings were important for children whatever their particular religious beliefs might be. When the case was appealed to the Kentucky Supreme Court, the Justices split their vote evenly. This allowed the lower court's decision to stand.

The parents took their case to the United States Supreme Court in 1980. The Court declared the Kentucky law unconstitutional, stating that it clearly had a religious purpose. But the Court also stated that posting the Commandments would "induce the schoolchildren to read, meditate upon, perhaps to venerate and obey, the Commandments." So those who wanted the Commandments to remain on the walls of the schools argued that the Court's ruling did not ban them; it merely made them voluntary instead of mandatory.

The state of New Hampshire had a similar situation concerning the words "In God We Trust." Parents challenged a state legislative resolution requiring a plaque with that motto to be hung in all schools. The state supreme court upheld the law, stating that the motto appeared on coins and in other nonreligious places, and that it did not single out one religion over another.

Can Students Receive Bibles and Other Religious Literature in Public Schools?

In the early 1950s, a New Jersey school district allowed students to accept Bibles from a religious group called the Gideon Society. This was done at the end of the school day, in a particular classroom. The children were required to receive permission from their parents before they could accept the Bibles. Some parents felt that the school district overstepped its authority by allowing distribution of the Bibles. In a sense, the school was supporting and advancing religion. Ultimately the case made it to the New Jersey Supreme Court, which ruled in favor of the parents. It determined that peer pressure made the students feel obligated to accept the Bibles. Their constitutional rights were being violated. The United States Supreme Court refused to hear the case and any other cases involving the same issue.

9

Religious Issues Outside of School

Can Cities Use Religious Ceremonies and Displays?

In the early 1980s, a Nativity scene, also known as a crèche, was an important part of a holiday display presented by the city of Pawtucket, Rhode Island. But not everyone enjoyed it. Some citizens, joined by the American Civil Liberties Union, protested by taking the city to court. They argued that their First Amendment rights were violated. It became a heated issue, with then-President Reagan strongly urging the city to allow the use of the Nativity scene.

The Supreme Court decided that the use of the

crèche should be allowed to continue. Chief Justice Warren Burger wrote that the Court cannot require complete separation of church and state. It does require "accommodation, not merely tolerance, of all religions, and forbids hostility toward any."[1] The Court went on to state that the purpose of the Nativity scene was not totally religious. It also depicted "the historical origins" of this national holiday.

The Supreme Court felt differently when faced with the situation of a Christmas Nativity scene placed at the entrance to the Allegheny County Courthouse in Pennsylvania. Since there were no other nonreligious displays along with the Nativity scene, the Court ruled that it was clearly an endorsement of Christianity. This was a violation of the Establishment Clause.

The Court took yet a different stand when considering a display that included a Christmas tree, a sign honoring freedom, and an eighteen-foot Chanukah menorah in front of a government building. Because citizens would not view such a display as either supporting or discouraging any particular religion, said the Court, no Establishment Clause rights were violated.

Can Religious Oaths Be Required before Taking Public Office?

Atheist Ray Torcaso was appointed as a notary public

A crèche, or Nativity scene, is a display of the celebration of the birth of Jesus, with the Virgin Mary, Joseph, shepherds, and the Wise Men bearing gifts. Its display on government property created quite a controversy in Pawtucket, Rhode Island, and other cities.

in the state of Maryland in 1961. But he refused to take his oath of office when he realized it meant he had to declare a belief in God. He sued the state of Maryland for requiring such an oath. He won the unanimous support of the United States Supreme Court, which declared that the state could not require a person to profess a religious belief or the lack of one.

Must an Alien Take a Naturalization Oath before Becoming a Citizen?

When someone wants to become an American citizen, he or she is required to take an oath, promising to "support and defend the Constitution and the law of the United States of America against all enemies foreign and domestic." This was perceived as a promise to bear arms, and several applicants who opposed war for religious purposes chose not to make such a promise. Therefore, they were turned down for citizenship, despite the fact that they met every other requirement.

At first the Supreme Court upheld the government's right to require the oath. But in the mid-1940s, the Court changed its mind. It decided that the oath didn't necessarily require an applicant to be willing to bear arms and enter combat.

Can Individuals Be Excused from Military Service Because of Their Religious Beliefs?

There are several religious groups that oppose war or any kind of armed conflict. These groups include the Amish, the Mennonites, and the Brethren. When the United States conducts a military draft during wartime, those who are opposed to combat on grounds of religion or moral conscience can apply for "conscientious objector (or CO) status," so that they don't have to fight.

One of the most publicized cases of a "CO" attempting to avoid serving in the Army involved heavyweight boxing champion Muhammad Ali. Ali was a minister in a politically active black religious group called the Nation of Islam. When he was born in 1942, he was named Cassius Clay, but he took on the Muslim name of Muhammad Ali when he joined the group in 1964. That same year he beat Sonny Liston for the world heavyweight championship. But the crown was taken away in 1967 when he refused to serve in the Army for religious reasons. In addition, he was arrested for draft evasion and later convicted. The United States government argued that Ali was merely trying to avoid going to war. It said that the Nation of Islam was a political group fostering black power and was not a religious sect.

95

Ali appealed the conviction to the United States Supreme Court and won in 1971. The draft was ended in 1973, but in the event of another large-scale war it may be reinstituted. The question of conscientious objectors will most assuredly arise again.

Can Churches Be Excused from Paying Taxes?

In 1980, New York property owner Frederick Walz didn't like the fact that he was required to pay taxes while churches were not. He argued that those individuals and businesses that were required to pay taxes were, in a sense, contributing involuntarily to the tax-exempt churches. This was a violation of the establishment of religion protection provided by the First Amendment.

The United States Supreme Court disagreed. It stated that tax exemptions do not constitute state support of a church. In fact, the Court wrote, such an exemption means less government involvement because it eliminates the need for tax assessments and other legal entanglements such as foreclosures and liens.

Can State Laws Force Stores to Be Closed on Sunday?

Pennsylvania as well as other states have long had so-called Blue Laws, prohibiting businesses and retail

A property owner in New York resented the fact that churches were tax-exempt, and didn't have to pay taxes. He called it an infringement of the First Amendment's Establishment Clause.

stores from operating on Sundays. Such laws were instituted so that everyone would observe one day of rest together.

One Orthodox Jew, a Mr. Braunfeld, regularly closed his clothing store on the Jewish Sabbath, Saturday, but he wanted to be open on Sundays. This was prohibited by the local Blue Laws. He sued the state, maintaining that his right to exercise his religion was being violated.

The United States Supreme Court disagreed. It ruled in 1961 that the Sunday closing laws were not instituted for religious reasons, and did not interfere with anyone's right to practice his religion.

Can the State Refuse to Pay Unemployment Benefits If a Worker Refuses to Work on Her Sabbath?

The Court changed its mind two years later in *Sherbert* v. *Verner*, a 1963 South Carolina case. Adell Sherbert, a Seventh Day Adventist, worked in a textile mill. Seventh Day Adventists believe that Christ will return in person. They observe the Sabbath on Saturday, the seventh day. When Adell was asked to work on Saturdays, she refused because of her religious beliefs. She was fired, and was denied unemployment benefits.

American workers receive unemployment benefits when they have been fired or laid off and have been unable to find comparable work. A worker cannot receive unemployment benefits, however, if he or she has turned down available work. Because Adell Sherbert refused the work she was offered on Saturdays, her Sabbath, the state of South Carolina denied her the benefits.

The Supreme Court ruled in Ms. Sherbert's favor. It stated that denying her those benefits forced her unfairly to make a choice between observing her strong religious beliefs or receiving unemployment compensation.

Justice William J. Brennan, Jr., stated that the only way that the state could deny Ms. Sherbert her religious beliefs was if there was a "compelling state interest"—for instance, the state felt she was committing fraud in order to receive benefits. But, Ms. Sherbert was not avoiding available work and was not attempting to commit fraud. Justice Brennan stated in his opinion that requiring Ms. Sherbert to make a choice between observing her religious beliefs and collecting unemployment benefits was just like making her pay a fine to go to church on Sunday.

Can the State Forbid Bigamy and Polygamy Even If They Are Religious Practices?

Every state has a law allowing each individual to be married to only one person at a time. Being married to two people at the same time is called bigamy; being married to several people at the same time is polygamy. In 1879, a member of the Mormon church in Utah argued before the United States Supreme Court that the restrictions against polygamy violated his right to freely exercise his Mormon beliefs, which supported multiple marriages. (In fact, the Mormon practice of being married to several people at once delayed Utah's admission as a state until 1896.)

The Supreme Court disagreed with the Mormon philosophy. It found it impossible to believe that the guarantee of religious freedom was meant to prevent legislation governing marriage. The Court went even further eleven years later in *Davis* v. *Beason.* This case involved an Idaho law that denied the right to vote to men who had more than one spouse. The Court said that the laws against polygamy were designed to support the stability of the family and its morals, and that the free exercise of religion must stand in line behind those laws.

10

After Engel and Beyond

The school prayer issue didn't end with *Engel* v. *Vitale* in 1962. It returned to the Supreme Court again in 1985. Ishmael Jaffree, the father of two second graders and a kindergarten student, brought a lawsuit against a school board in Mobile, Alabama. Jaffree argued that his children were receiving religious instruction and were asked to pray together in school. The state of Alabama had a law that allowed a moment of silence each morning.

The Supreme Court ruled against the Mobile school board and silent prayer, saying it failed the "purpose test." Was the purpose of the law to advance religion? In the majority opinion, Justice John P. Stevens stated that he believed the intent of the law was "to return prayer to the schools," and that its only purpose was to advance religion.

An interesting point was made in the dissenting opinion written by Justice William H. Rehnquist. Opposing the majority opinion, he wrote that the concept of a wall of separation used in determining cases was useless and should be "abandoned." His remarks were in the minority, but they signaled the beginning of the Court's softening on the strict barrier between church and state.

School prayer became an issue once again in June of 1989. Fourteen-year-old Deborah Weisman was preparing to graduate from Nathan Bishop Middle School in Providence, Rhode Island. When she and her father, Daniel Weisman, learned that a rabbi would be delivering prayers at the beginning and end of the graduation ceremony, they asked the federal district court to prevent it. With only four days left before the ceremony, the court refused to prohibit the prayers on the grounds that it lacked enough time to carefully consider both sides of the issue.

The rabbi did deliver the prayers. Both began with the word "God" and ended with "Amen." Deborah and her father, unhappy with the religious ceremony being forced upon them, went back to court. This time they

This is the conference room in which the country's highest court makes its major decisions. Security is so tight that no one other than the Justices is permitted inside the room during discussions.

asked that prayers be prohibited from all graduation and promotion ceremonies in public schools.

Not only did they win their case in the federal district court, but the United States Supreme Court upheld the decision. It ruled that it was unfair to students to have to choose between tolerating a religious ceremony or not attending their own graduation. The Court also relied on its earlier decision in *Engel* v. *Vitale*.

Just one year later, the high court seemed to be softening its position on prayers at graduation ceremonies. On July 7, 1993, the Court allowed a lower court decision to stand. This decision permitted prayers at graduation ceremonies in Texas, Louisiana, and Mississippi. The ruling did not affect schools in other states, but it displayed a major shift in the Court's attitude toward permitting religious activity in schools.

On the very same day, the Court issued a related ruling. It required schools to allow religious groups to hold meetings on their property, if they also permit its use by other community and nonreligious groups. A religious group from Lamb's Chapel in the town of Center Moriches, New York, had requested permission from school officials to use the school auditorium to show Christian films. When the school turned them down for reasons of separation of church and state, Lamb's Chapel went all the way to the high court. The

Court stated that the school has the right to deny access to all groups but it cannot single out the religious ones.

The Supreme Court had ruled on the issue of religious meetings in the past. In the 1981 *Widmar* v. *Vincent* case, the Court ruled that the University of Missouri had violated a student's constitutional right to freedom of religion. The university had refused to allow him to hold a religious meeting in a building on campus without being able to show a compelling state interest. But the *Widmar* decision addressed the issue of worship services in colleges. The Lamb's Chapel case is the most recent one that answered the same question for high schools.

In June 1993, the United States Supreme Court had refused to hear an atheist's attempt to challenge the use of the Pledge of Allegiance in elementary schools. Robert Sherman of Wheeling Township, Illinois, objected to the pledge because it refers to "one nation under God." An appeals court ruled against Sherman, stating that because the pledge is repeated over and over again, its words have become a ceremony rather than having a significant religious meaning.

The Court seems to have ruled in a similar manner in cases not involving schools. In 1983, Ernest Chambers, a Nebraska Congressman, was angered by the fact that each session of the state legislature began with a prayer from a Presbyterian chaplain. The chaplain was paid $319.75 a month during the time the legislature was in session. Congressman Chambers sued the state, arguing that the Establishment Clause was being violated.

The Supreme Court ruled in favor of the chaplain and the prayer. It said that the practice of paying the chaplain to pray before the legislative session began during the Continental Congress. It has since become tradition with all other sessions of Congress. Several of the early colonies that championed religious freedom allowed paid chaplains to open their legislatures, and so do most states today.

The Court also pointed out that appointing paid chaplains was authorized by Congress three days after the Bill of Rights was approved. Apparently, the Founding Fathers did not see the act of paying chaplains as a conflict with the right to freedom of religion.

Historically, Supreme Court rulings have indicated a strong policy of separating church and schools and church and government. It appears, however, that the American people often don't share the Court's feelings.

In 1991, *Time* magazine and CNN (Cable News Network) conducted a telephone poll of American adults about religion in schools and in everyday life.[1] Seventy-eight percent of those polled said that they favored allowing children to pray in school; 18 percent were opposed. Eighty-nine percent supported a moment of silent meditation; only 9 percent opposed it. Sixty-seven percent expressed support for displaying symbols such as a Nativity scene or a Chanukah menorah on government property, while 26 percent opposed it. Only 20 percent felt that any references to God should be removed from all oaths of public office; 74 percent opposed their removal.

Results of a 1992 poll conducted by *Reader's Digest* magazine showed little change in public sentiment.[2] Seventy-five percent of those asked said that they favored prayer in public schools, with only 19 percent opposing it.[3] Eighty percent disapproved of the Court's decision declaring prayers at school graduations to be unconstitutional, with only 18 percent approving. When asked how they felt about setting up Nativity scenes or Chanukah menorahs during the holiday season, 76 percent felt the practice was acceptable; 21 percent said it was not. Fifty-nine percent of those in the poll said they would be more likely to vote for a presidential or congressional candidate who supported school prayer; 16 percent said they would be less likely to vote for such a candidate.

School prayer, Bible-reading, and the other issues involving separation of church and state started to reach the United States Supreme Court in 1947, but the debate has still only just begun. The makeup of the Supreme Court continues to change. New Justices with different views and different interpretations will determine the part that religion will play in our schools and in our lives.

As we trace how the Justices have decided these explosive issues over the past five decades, we can see that at times they have based their decisions on what they believe the intent of the writers of the Bill of Rights to have been. Yet, in other instances, they have used a three-part test. They determined a law to be unconstitutional if it has only religious purposes, if its primary effect is to advance or inhibit religion, or if the government becomes excessively entangled with religion.

In the decades to come, the Supreme Court will be called upon to address these religious issues as well as all kinds of new ones. It will be interesting to see how our changing values and morals will affect these most important decisions.

You Be the Judge

Now you know the arguments that both sides presented. You know some of the reasoning behind the arguments. And you know how the Justices decided. But remember, this took place back in 1962, more than thirty years ago. Let's re-enact the whole situation, using the same facts as well as your imagination. So that everyone has a part in this, divide your class into groups:

Justices

There were nine Justices who heard oral arguments on April 3, 1962, but two did not vote—Justices Frankfurter and White. Select students to role-play each of the Justices who participated.

- Chief Justice Earl Warren

- Justice Hugo Black
- Justice William O. Douglas
- Justice Potter Stewart
- Justice Tom C. Clark
- Justice William J. Brennan, Jr.
- Justice John M. Harlan

Attorneys

Three attorneys were permitted to present oral arguments.

- William Butler represented Engel and the other parents as well as the New York branch of the American Civil Liberties Union.
- Bertram B. Daiker was the attorney for the New Hyde Park School Board.
- Porter C. Chandler provided legal representation to the Board of Regents as well as to the sixteen parents who joined on the side of the school board.

Weeks before the attorneys appear before the Supreme Court to present oral arguments, they are required to submit briefs, their arguments in written form. In this way, the Justices have an opportunity to familiarize themselves with the case before it is presented to them orally. Students can work together, one presenting oral arguments with another preparing the brief for each side.

Briefs may also be presented by others who are not parties to the case. Someone presenting such a brief is called an amicus curiae, or "friend of the court." Those submitting briefs in the *Engel* case included:

- the American Jewish Committee against the prayer.

- the Synagogue Council of America against the prayer.

- attorneys general from nineteen states in support of prayer.

Each brief should be relatively short, a few pages, and should be very well organized. Remember that the goal of a brief is to convince the Justices that your arguments make the most sense. Attorneys and their law clerks will often spend days in law libraries looking up cases that had similar circumstances and that ended with a decision as close as possible to the one they are trying to achieve.

You will find that the preparation of the brief will help you develop your oral argument. Each side is permitted only thirty minutes to present its case. Try not to read from a prepared statement. Instead, try to discuss the case, referring only to an outline. Each "attorney" should prepare a presentation and be ready to answer questions asked by the "Justices."

Chief Justice WIlliam Rehnquist's dissenting opinion in *Wallace* v. *Jaffree* served as a signal that the Court may have been softening its tough stance against prayers at school events.

The students assigned to the roles of the Justices should prepare questions and try to put the attorneys on the spot. You may want to use some of the questions suggested at the end of this chapter.

After briefs have been written and submitted and the oral arguments have been presented, have the Justices go to another room.

Follow the procedure actually used in the United States Supreme Court—the Justice who has been on the Court the longest begins by presenting his views and concerns. In this case it would be Justice Black. He has unlimited time to speak and is then followed by the next in line of seniority, Justice Douglas, then Justice Clark, Chief Justice Warren, followed by Justices Harlan, Brennan, and Stewart.

This continues until all nine, or in this case seven, have a chance to speak, ask and answer questions, and exchange ideas. The transcripts from the oral arguments as well as the written briefs are considered and referred to.

Then it's time to vote. The Justice with least seniority goes first. This is done to avoid giving the impression that his decision was influenced by a more experienced Justice. The voting continues until a majority vote is reached.

Don't worry if the decision made by your Court

The future of school prayer as well as other church and state matters rests with the Justices who currnetly sit on the United States Supreme Court and those who will replace them over the decades and the centuries to come.

differs from the one reached in 1962. The Constitution was drafted so that the law changes with the times. As we said earlier, it's possible that the Justices sitting on today's Supreme Court might deal quite differently with the school prayer issue than did the Warren Court.

After a decision has been reached, one of the Justices voting with the majority should be appointed to write the majority opinion. In the *Engel* case, it was Justice Hugo Black. Concurring or agreeing opinions can also be written. They arrive at the same conclusion as the majority opinion, but may present a different reason or add a few points.

If anyone has taken the minority view, he or she should write the dissenting or disagreeing opinion.

When all of the opinions have been written and copied, they should be circulated among the Justices. Each justice is permitted to make suggestions in what will become the final decision of the Court.

When the opinions are completed and approved by everyone, the majority opinion is read in open court. In the *Engel* case, it was read by Justice Black. The job of the Justices is now completed for this case; the judgment they have reached is final.

Other issues that the class can consider or that can be used as questions by the Justices when oral arguments are presented to them:

1. Examining the prayer phrase by phrase, did it establish a religion? To what groups could it have been offensive?

2. In 1971, the Supreme Court, in *Lemon v. Kurtzman,* established three criteria for determining if a law was unconstitutional. Take the situation of the *Engel* case and determine if any of the three apply:

    (a) It cannot have a religious governmental function.

    (b) It can neither advance nor inhibit religion.

    (c) It cannot support the government's becoming excessively entangled with religion.

3. Is a belief that there is no God really a religion?

4. Does the Court's decision against school prayer actually interfere with anyone's right to practice their religion?

5. How do you think previous Court decisions influenced the decision in *Engel v. Vitale*?

6. What was the intent of our Founding Fathers when writing the First Amendment? Were they just trying to prevent the establishment of a single church (as in England) or of all religions?

7. Was the Regents' Prayer really voluntary or were students pressured into participating?

8. Should other religious practices be eliminated, such as prayer before a session of Congress?

9. Should other references to God and religion be removed from things related to the government, such as the printing on coins and bills of "In God We Trust"?

10. If you had been one of the students whose parents objected to the prayer, would you have wanted your parents to ignore it and not challenge it?

11. Was the negative treatment of the plaintiffs by other students and parents justified?

12. Did the Supreme Court decision mean that all kinds of prayer were prohibited in schools? How about meditation?

13. What effect do you think *Engel* v. *Vitale* will have on future decisions about prayer in the schools?

14. Do you believe that the thinking regarding prayer in the schools has changed considerably since 1962?

These are only suggested questions for discussion. Put yourselves in the place of the students, parents, or members of smaller religious denominations, and see what new issues arise.

Chapter Notes

Chapter 1

1. *Engel* v. *Vitale*, 370 U.S. 421 (1962).

Chapter 2

1. *Abington School District* v. *Schempp*, 374 U.S. 241 (1963).

2. *Everson* v. *Board of Education*, 330 U.S. 1 (1947).

3. Ibid.

Chapter 3

1. *Engel* v. *Vitale*, 370 U.S. 421 (1962).

Chapter 5

1. "Still In The Storm's Center," *Time*, July 6, 1962, p. 9.

2. *Engel* v. *Vitale*, 370 U.S. 421 (1962).

3. *Zorach* v. *Clauson*, 343 U.S. 306 (1952).

Chapter 6

1. Anthony Lewis, "Congressmen Act to Overrule Court," *The New York Times*, June 26, 1962, p. 16.

2. Paul Blanshard, *Religion and the Schools: The Great Controversy* (Boston: Beacon Press, 1963), p. 50.

3. "The Supreme Court—To Stand as a Guarantee," *Time*, July 6, 1962, p. 8.

4. "Prayer Ruling Debated," *Christian Science Monitor*, June 26, 1962, p. 4.

5. Ibid.

6. *Atlanta Journal-Constitution*, June 28, 1962, p. 1.

7. Alexander Burnham, "Edict Is Called a Setback by Christian Clerics," *The New York Times*, June 26, 1962, p. 17.

8. Ibid., p. 1.

9. Ibid., p. 17.

10. Fred Hechinger, "Many States Use Prayer in School," *The New York Times*, June 26, 1962, p. 17.

11. Roy Silver, "Five L.I. Parents Who Started Suit Hail Decision," *The New York Times*, June 25, 1962, p. 1.

12. John H. Laubach, *School Prayers: Congress, the Courts, and the Public* (Washington, D.C.:Public Affairs Press), 1969, p. 47.

13. Ibid., p. 85.

14. Becker Hearings, U.S. Congress, House of Representatives, Committee of the Judiciary, "School Prayers," Hearings before the Committee on the Judiciary, House of Representatives, 88th Congress, 2nd session, 1964, p. 937, cited in Laubach, p. 63.

15. Ibid., p. 242, cited in Laubach, p. 64.

16. Laubach, p. 94.

17. John Noble Wilford, "Crew of Apollo Eight Is Saluted by President and Congress," *The New York Times*, January 10, 1969, p. 30.

18. Ibid.

Chapter 7
No Notes.

Chapter 8

1. *West Virginia State Board of Education* v. *Barnett,* 319 U.S. 624 (1943).

2. *School District of Abington Township* v. *Schempp, Murray* v. *Curlett,* 374 U.S. 203 (1963).

3. *Funk & Wagnalls New Encyclopedia,* Vol. 1 (New York: Funk & Wagnalls, 1986), p. 147.

4. Ibid.

Chapter 9

1. *Pierce* v. *Society of Sisters,* 268 U.S. 510 (1925).

2. Ibid.

3. *Rice* v. *Commonwealth of Virginia,* 188 VA. 224 (1948).

4. *Funk & Wagnalls New Encyclopedia,* Vol. 2 (New York: Funk & Wagnalls, 1986), p. 89.

5. *Mitchell* v. *McCall,* 143 So. 2d 629 (Ala. 1962).

6. *Edwards* v. *Aguillard,* 482 U.S. 578 (1987).

7. *Board of Education of Central School District No 1* v. *Allen,* 392 U.S. 236 (1968).

8. *Stone* v. *Graham,* 449 U.S. 39 (1980).

Chapter 10

1. *Lynch* v. *Donnelly,* 465 U.S. 668 (1984).

Chapter 11

1. Nancy Gibbs, "America's Holy War," *Time,* December 9, 1991, p. 64.

2. Eugene H. Methvin, "Let Us Pray," *Reader's Digest,* November, 1992, p.75.

3. Ibid.

Glossary

abstain—To refrain from voting, as did Justices Frankfurter and White in the *Engel* decision.

amicus curiae—A "friend of the court," usually groups or individuals that are interested in the outcome of a case but are not parties to it.

atheist—A nonbeliever in a God or a higher being.

Bill of Rights—The first ten amendments to the U. S. Constititution, ratified three years after the original Preamble and seven articles.

Blue Laws—State laws that prohibit retail stores from opening on Sundays.

brief—A written document that states the arguments an attorney wants to make in his case.

child benefit theory—An argument used by the courts to permit a religious activity, based on the thinking that it is the children who are gaining benefits from the activity, not the church or school.

concurring opinion—An opinion written in a case that agrees with the majority opinion but adds different or additional reasons for reaching the same conclusion.

creationism—The theory that the universe was created by a Supreme Being in seven days as detailed in the Book of Genesis.

crèche—A Nativity scene, re-creating the celebration of the birth of Jesus Christ.

defendant—The person or party being sued.

dissenting opinion—A written statement that expresses the opinion of the Justice or Justices not voting with the majority opinion.

Establishment Clause—One of two parts of the clause in the First Amendment granting religious freedom, stating that the government is prohibited from favoring one religion over another or from sponsoring a church or religion.

Ethical Culture Society—A movement that originated in New York City in 1876; it stresses strong ethics and morals rather than a strict religious doctrine.

evolution—The theory that the entire universe is in a process of gradual evolution dating back millions of years to the Big Bang, running contrary to the teachings of the Bible that God created man in one day.

First Amendment—The first of ten amendments added to the Constitution in 1791. It provides freedom of religion, speech, press, and petitioning the government.

Free-Exercise Clause—One of two parts of the religion clause in the First Amendment. It prohibits the government from passing laws that place burdens on individuals because of their religious beliefs.

House Judiciary Committee—One of the most powerful committees in the House of Representatives. It can control whether a bill is "tabled" or set aside, or whether it moves on for a vote to the full House.

immunization—A vaccination or inoculation given, often to school-aged children, to prevent whooping cough, diphtheria, tuberculosis, or other diseases.

injunction—A court order that requires an individual to perform a particular act or prohibits him from doing one.

Jehovah's Witnesses—A religious sect that believes in the Second Coming of Christ and refuses to salute the flag or join the armed services.

Ku Klux Klan—An organization that opposes ethnic groups that are not Protestant Caucasians, particularly blacks, but also Catholics, Jews, Asians, and Hispanics.

majority opinion—When the Justices of the United States Supreme Court vote on a case, the majority decision is written by one of the Justices and becomes the "majority opinion."

menorah—In the Jewish faith, a candlestick holding nine candles lit during the religious holiday of Chanukah.

Mormons—Also known as the Church of Jesus Christ of Latter-Day Saints, this religious group was founded in 1830 by Joseph Smith. Until the late nineteenth century, they believed in men being married to more than one wife at a time.

oral arguments—The presentation each attorney makes to the Court, outlining the reasons why the Justices should rule in his or her client's favor.

Pentecostal faith—A Protestant religious faith that

believes in faith healing and the Second Coming of Christ.

plaintiff—The person bringing the lawsuit and suing the defendant.

released time—Time during the school day in which students were dismissed from school to attend religious instruction off school property. It was the basis of a lawsuit in 1952.

Seventh Day Adventists—Founded in 1863, this religious sect believes in the Second Coming of Christ and is the largest group of Adventists.

tax exemption—The status that a group, such as a church, is granted by the government, to be free from paying taxes.

unemployment compensation—Money that the state pays individuals for a short period of time when they are unable to find work.

Unitarian Church—A Christian religious group that does not believe in the Trinity of the Father, Son, and Holy Ghost. Instead, they believe in God's existence as one individual.

wall of separation of church and state—An interpretation of the religion clause of the First Amendment to mean that there is a barrier between church and state. Some scholars and Justices believe it is an inpenetrable wall; others believe there are times when the wall should be "lowered" and some religious practices be permitted.

Further Reading

Alley, Robert S., ed. *The Supreme Court On Church And State*. New York: Oxford University Press, 1988.

Blanshard, Paul. *Religion and the Schools: The Great Controversy*. Boston: Beacon Press, 1963.

Boles, Donald E. *The Bible, Religion, and the Public Schools*. Ames, Iowa: Iowa State University Press, 1965.

Cord, Robert L. *Separation of Church and State*. New York: Lambeth Press, 1982.

Cox, Claire. *The Fourth R*. New York: Hawthorn Books, 1969.

Garraty, John A., ed. *Quarrels That Have Shaped The Constitution*. New York: Harper & Row, 1987.

Irons, Peter. *The Courage of Their Convictions*. New York: Free Press, 1988.

Laubach, John. *School Prayers: Congress, The Courts, and the Public*. Washington, D.C.: Public Affairs Press, 1969.

McCarthy, Martha M. *A Delicate Balance: Church, State, and the Schools*. Bloomington, IN.: Indiana University Press, 1983.

Pfeffer, Leo. *Religion, State and the Burger Court*. Buffalo, N.Y.: Prometheus, 1984.

Schimmel, David. *Parents, Schools and the Law.* Columbia, Md.: National Committee for Citizens in Education, 1987.

Witt, Elder. *The Supreme Court and Individual Rights.* Washington, D.C.: Congressional Quarterly, 1988.

Index